Hot Math Topics

Problem Solving, Communication, and Reasoning

Number Sense

grade
1

Carole E. Greenes
Linda Schulman Dacey
Rika Spungin

Dale Seymour Publications®
White Plains, New York

This book is published by Dale Seymour Publications®,
an imprint of Addison Wesley Longman, Inc.

Dale Seymour Publications
10 Bank Street
White Plains, New York 10602
Customer Service: 800-872-1100

Managing Editor: Catherine Anderson
Senior Editor: John Nelson
Project Editor: Mali Apple
Production/Manufacturing Director: Janet Yearian
Sr. Production/Manufacturing Coordinator: Fiona Santoianni
Design Director: Phyllis Aycock
Text and Cover Design: Tracey Munz
Cover and Interior Illustrations: Jared Lee
Composition: Alan Noyes

DALE SEYMOUR PUBLICATIONS®

Order number 21871
ISBN 0-7690-0013-4

1 2 3 4 5 6 7 8 9 10-ML-02 01 00 99 98

This Book Is Printed
On Recycled Paper

contents

Introduction

Why Was *Hot Math Topics* Developed?

The *Hot Math Topics* series was developed for several reasons:

- to offer children practice and mainte-nance of previously learned skills and concepts
- to enhance problem solving and mathematical reasoning abilities
- to build literacy skills
- to nurture collaborative learning behaviors

Practicing and maintaining concepts and skills

Although textbooks and core curriculum materials do treat the topics explored in this series, their treatment is often limited by the lesson format and the page size. As a consequence, there are often not enough opportunities for children to practice newly acquired concepts and skills related to the topics, or to connect the topics to other content areas. *Hot Math Topics* provides the necessary practice and mathematical connections.

Similarly, core instructional programs often do not do a very good job of helping children maintain their skills. Although textbooks do include reviews of previously learned material, they are frequently limited to sidebars or boxed-off areas on one or two pages in each chapter, with four or five exercises in each box. Each set of problems is intended only as a sampling of previously taught topics, rather than as a complete review. In the selection and placement of the review exercises, little or no attention is given to levels of complexity of the problems. By contrast, *Hot Math Topics* targets specific topics and gives children more experience with concepts and skills related to them. The problems are sequenced by difficulty, allowing children to hone their skills. And, because they are not tied to specific lessons, the problems can be used at any time.

Enhancing problem solving and mathematical reasoning abilities

Hot Math Topics presents children with situations in which they may use a variety of problem solving strategies, including

- designing and conducting experiments to generate or collect data
- guessing, checking, and revising guesses
- organizing data in lists or tables in order to identify patterns and relationships
- choosing appropriate computational algorithms and deciding on a sequence of computations
- using inverse operations in "work backward" solution paths

For their solutions, children are also required to bring to bear various methods of reasoning, including

- deductive reasoning
- inductive reasoning
- proportional reasoning

For example, to solve clue-type problems, children must reason deductively and make inferences about mathematical relationships in order to generate candidates for the solutions and to home in on those that meet all of the problem's conditions.

To identify and continue a pattern and then write a rule for finding the next term in that pattern, children must reason inductively.

To compute unit prices and convert measurement units, children must reason proportionally.

To estimate or compare magnitudes of numbers, or to determine the type of number appropriate for a given situation, children must apply their number sense skills.

Building communication and literacy skills

Hot Math Topics offers children opportunities to write and talk about mathematical ideas. For many problems, children must describe their solution paths, justify their solutions, give their opinions, or write or tell stories.

Some problems have multiple solution methods. With these problems, children may have to compare their methods with those of their peers and talk about how their approaches are alike and different.

Other problems have multiple solutions, requiring children to confer to be sure they have found all possible answers.

Nurturing collaborative learning behaviors

Several of the problems can be solved by children working together. Some are designed specifically as partner problems. By working collaboratively, children can develop expertise in posing questions that call for clarification or verification, brainstorming solution strategies, and following another person's line of reasoning.

What Is in *Number Sense*?

This book contains 100 problems and tasks that focus on number concepts and operations with numbers. The mathematics content, the mathematical connections, the problem solving strategies, and the communication skills that are emphasized are described below.

Mathematics content

Number sense problems and tasks require children to

- count, count on, and skip count
- compare and estimate quantities
- identify place values of digits
- know the meaning of numbers and of operations with numbers
- add and subtract—basic facts and multiples of 10
- use one-to-one and one-to-many correspondence
- create equal groups (in preparation for multiplication and division)
- identify values of collections of pennies, nickels, and dimes
- identify uses of numbers in real-world situations
- identify the relative magnitudes of numbers that correspond to real-world situations

Mathematical connections

In these problems and tasks, connections are made to these other topic areas:

- measurement
- money
- algebra
- geometry
- graphs

Problem solving strategies

Number Sense problems and tasks offer children opportunities to use one or more of several problem solving strategies.

- **Formulate Questions and Stories:** When data are presented in displays or text form, children must pose one or more questions that can be answered using the given data or create stories using the data.

- **Complete Stories:** When confronted with an incomplete story, children must supply the missing information and then check that the story makes sense.

- **Organize Information:** To ensure that several solution candidates for a problem are considered, children may have to organize information by drawing a picture, making a list, or constructing a bar graph or a table.

- **Guess, Check, and Revise:** In some problems, children have to identify candidates for the solution and then check whether those candidates match the conditions of the problem. If the conditions are not satisfied, other possible solutions must be generated and verified.

- **Identify and Continue Patterns:** To identify the next term or terms in a sequence, children have to recognize the relationship between successive terms and then generalize that relationship.

- **Use Logic:** Children have to reason deductively, from clues, to make inferences about the solution to a problem. They have to reason inductively to continue numeric patterns.

- **Work Backward:** In some problems, the output is given and children must determine the input by identifying mathematical relationships between the input and output and applying inverse operations.

Communication skills

Problems and tasks in *Number Sense* are designed to stimulate communication. As part of the solution process, children may have to

- describe their thinking steps
- describe patterns and rules
- find alternate solution methods and solution paths
- identify other possible answers
- formulate problems for classmates to solve
- compare estimates, solutions, and methods with classmates
- make drawings to clarify mathematical relationships

These communication skills are enhanced when children interact with one another and with the teacher. By communicating both orally and in writing, children develop their understanding and use of the language of mathematics.

How Can *Hot Math Topics* Be Used?

The problems may be used as practice of newly learned concepts and skills, as maintenance of previously learned ideas, and as enrichment experiences for early finishers or more advanced students.

They may be used in class or given to children to take home and do with their families. If used during class, they may be selected to complement lessons dealing with a specific topic or assigned every week as a means of keeping skills alive and well.

For children whom the reading requirements of the problems exceed their current abilities, you may wish to use the problems in whole-class or group settings, where either you or an able reader presents the problems aloud.

As they become more able readers, children can work on the problems in pairs or on their own. The problems are sequenced from least to most difficult. The selection of problems may be made by the teacher or the children based on their needs or interests. If the plan is for children to choose problems, you may wish to copy individual problems onto card stock and laminate them, and establish a problem card file.

To facilitate record keeping, a Management Chart is provided on page 6. The chart can be duplicated so that there is one for each child. As a problem is completed, the space corresponding to that problem's number may be shaded. An Award Certificate is included on page 6 as well.

How Can Children's Performance Be Assessed?

Number Sense problems and tasks provide you with opportunities to assess children's

- knowledge of number, number concepts, and number relationships
- problem solving abilities
- mathematical reasoning methods
- communication skills

Observations

Keeping anecdotal records helps you to remember important information you gain as you observe children at work. To make observations more manageable, limit each observation to a group of from four to six children or to one of the areas noted above. You may find that using index cards facilitates the recording process.

Discussions

Many of the *Number Sense* problems and tasks allow for multiple answers or may be solved in a variety of ways. This built-in richness motivates children to discuss their work with one another. Small groups or class discussions are appropriate. As children share their approaches to the problems, you will gain additional insights into their content knowledge, mathematical reasoning, and communication abilities.

Scoring responses

You may wish to holistically score children's responses to the problems and tasks. The simple scoring rubric below uses three levels: high, medium, and low.

High	Medium	Low
• Solution demonstrates that the child knows the concepts and skills.	• Solution demonstrates that the child has some knowledge of the concepts and skills.	• Solution shows that the child has little or no grasp of the concepts and skills.
• Solution is complete and thorough.	• Solution is complete.	• Solution is incomplete or contains major errors.
• The child communicates effectively.	• The child communicates somewhat clearly.	• The child does not communicate effectively.

Portfolios

Having children store their responses to the problems in *Hot Math Topics* portfolios allows them to see improvement in their work over time. You may want to have them choose examples of their best responses for inclusion in their permanent portfolios, accompanied by explanations as to why each was chosen.

Children and the assessment process

Involving children in the assessment process is central to the development of their abilities to reflect on their own work, to understand the assessment standards to which they are held accountable, and to take ownership for their own learning. Young children may find the reflective process difficult, but with your coaching, they can develop such skills.

Discussion may be needed to help children better understand your standards for performance. Ask children such questions as, "What does it mean to communicate *clearly*?" "What is a *complete* response?" Some children may want to use simple icons to score their responses, such as these characters:

What Additional Materials Are Needed?

Some manipulative materials are required for solving the problems in *Number Sense,* including beans, cubes, chips, three number cubes, hundreds grids or boards, paper plates, and play money (pennies, nickels, and dimes). Inch tape measures or yardsticks, and tiles of various shapes, may be helpful. Crayons and colored pencils and one-inch grid paper should be readily accessible. Calculators are required in one task, and they may be helpful to children in solving some of the other problems.

Management Chart

Name _____

When a problem or task is completed, shade the box with that number.

1	2	3	4	5	6	7	8	9	10
11	12	13	14	15	16	17	18	19	20
21	22	23	24	25	26	27	28	29	30
31	32	33	34	35	36	37	38	39	40
41	42	43	44	45	46	47	48	49	50
51	52	53	54	25	56	57	58	59	60
61	62	63	64	65	66	67	68	69	70
71	72	73	74	75	76	77	78	79	80
81	82	83	84	85	86	87	88	89	90
91	92	93	94	95	96	97	98	99	100

Award Certificate

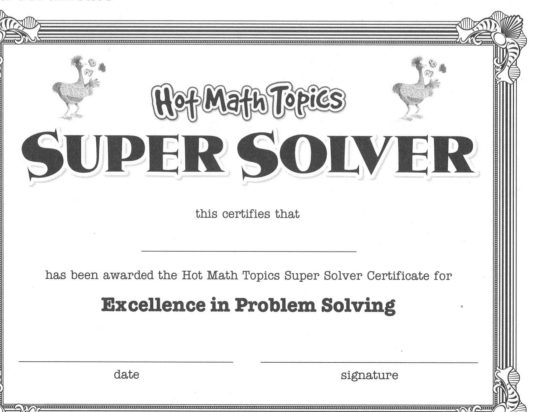

Hot Math Topics

SUPER SOLVER

this certifies that

_____

has been awarded the Hot Math Topics Super Solver Certificate for

Excellence in Problem Solving

_____   _____

date   signature

©Addison Wesley Longman, Inc./Published by Dale Seymour Publications®

©Addison-Wesley Publishing Company, Inc./Published by Dale Seymour Publications®

Problems and Tasks

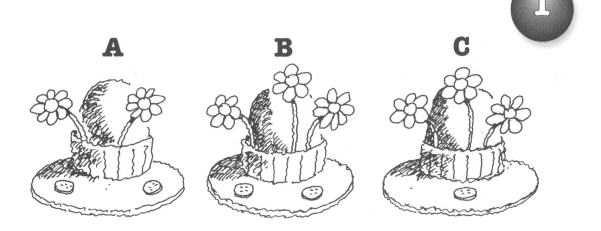

A   **B**   **C**

Mai's hat has 3 .

Mai's hat has 2 🥔 .

Which hat is Mai's?

- -

Talk with a friend.

Tell different ways to count
the bugs.

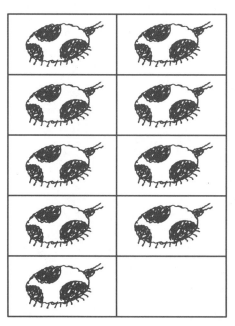

Draw 5 turtles in the water.

Draw 2 turtles on the rock.

How many turtles are there in all?

- -

Show someone that there is the same number of bananas as monkeys.

Use numbers to tell about the snowman.

Make a drawing.

- Draw 3 red balloons.
- Draw 2 blue balloons.
- Draw 1 more yellow balloon than red balloons.

There are _____ balloons in all.

Draw the picture that comes next.

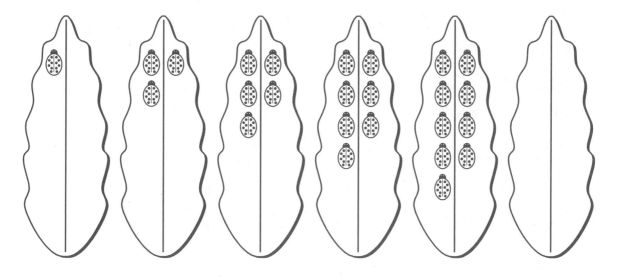

A **B** **C** **D**

Barry's kite has 4 ★.
Barry's kite has 2 〰.
Barry's kite has 5 ▰.
Which kite is Barry's?

Draw an X for each story Leah read.

She read a story about a singer.

She read 2 stories about whales.

She read 3 stories about clowns.

Leah read _____ stories.

9

- -

This is part of Cora's bead chain. There are 12 beads in all.

10

How many beads are ?
Tell how you know.

Get some chips.

Use one hand.
Take a bunch of chips.

Use the other hand.
Take a bunch of chips.

Match the chips,
one-to-one.

Which hand has
more chips?

Fill the shapes with numbers.

The story must make sense.

Lelia has ☐ baseball cards.

She has △ football cards.

She has ◯ more baseball
cards than football cards.

Draw 3 **on each** **.**

How many  **are there in all?**

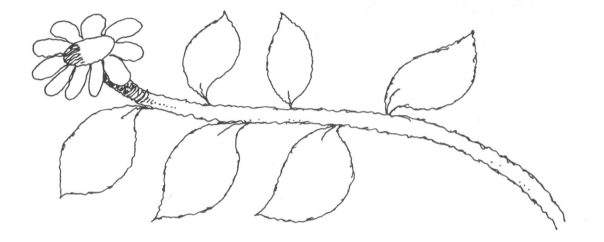

- -

Put some beans in A.

Put more beans in B than in A.

Put fewer beans in C than in A.

A	B	C

How many beans are there in all?

Draw 5 ants on the log.

Draw 2 ants on the leaf.

Draw 3 ants on the rock.

How many ants are there in all?

- -

Favorite Ice Cream

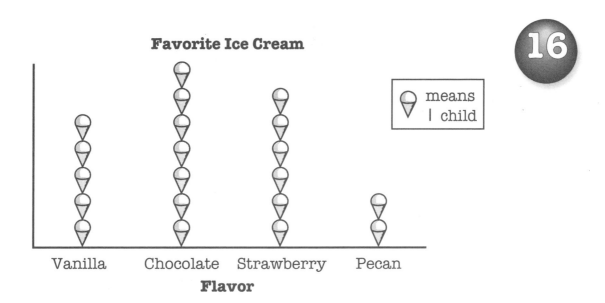

means
l child

Vanilla   Chocolate   Strawberry   Pecan

Flavor

Use the facts in the graph.

Write a story problem.

Have a classmate solve your problem.

There are 7 seals altogether.

How many seals are in the water?

Write numbers in the table to tell how many.

Animal	How Many?
duck	
turtle	
seal	
fish	

Write 2 questions about the table.

Make strips of 6 squares.

Use red and blue crayons.

Color to make different strips.

Write the numbers of red and blue squares.

_____ red   _____ blue

_____ red   _____ blue

_____ red   _____ blue

_____ red   _____ blue

_____ red   _____ blue

- -

Draw one line through the square.

**Put the same number of stars
on each side.**

How many stars are on each side?

Use these numbers.

4 435 25

Fill in numbers that make sense.

Number of children in a school. _____

Number of children in a class. _____

Number of children on the swings. _____

Play this game with a friend.

Get a bag of beans. Take turns.

Close your eyes. Try to take 10 beans.

Open your eyes. Count the beans.

Do you have more than, fewer than, or exactly 10 beans?

Play until one friend gets exactly 10 beans three times.

Play this game with a friend. Take turns.

Put fewer than 10 beans on the table.

Have your friend count the beans.

Use one hand. Cover some beans.

Don't let your friend see what you covered.

Ask, "How many beans did I cover?"

I started with 2.

I counted by ones.

I wrote the numbers.

The middle number I wrote was 10.

What was the greatest number I wrote?

Ask a friend to pick a number from 1 to 20.

Ask "yes" or "no" questions to guess the number.

Take turns.

Is your number greater than 10?

Robbie Rabbit has 2 + 1 buttons on his shirt.

Robbie Rabbit has 3 + 3 dots on his tie.

Which rabbit is Robbie?

A   B   C

Write a story about the animals.

Use the numbers in your story.

Use the words *more* or *fewer* in your story.

Use these sticker shapes.

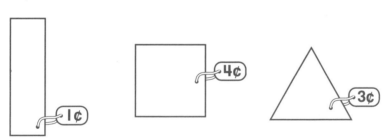

Draw an animal that costs more than 20¢.

Name your animal.

Tell how much your animal costs.

Work with 2 friends.

Each of you guess the number of chairs in your classroom.

Then count to find out how many chairs.

Number of Chairs

Name	Guess	Count
1.		
2.		
3.		

Who had the best guess?

- -

This is a + 4 pattern.

Fill in the numbers.

1, 5, 9, 13, ____, 21,

____, ____, ____, ____

Make up a + pattern.

Start with 2.

Give it to a friend to finish.

2, ____, ____, ____,

____, ____, ____, ____

Use a chip for each **in the story.**

Chickens on the Farm

12 were in the yard.

Some of the  went into the .

Now there are 5 chickens in the yard.

How many **went into the** **?**

- -

2   8   9   10

Which number does not belong?

Why?

Which number would you put in its place?

Why?

Write numbers that make sense.

Birds in the Trees

_____ 🐦 are on the 🌿 .

_____ 🐦 fly away.

_____ more 🐦 come to the 🌿 .

Now there are _____ 🐦 on the 🌿 .

You have .

Can you buy 2 bananas and I apple?

Tell why.

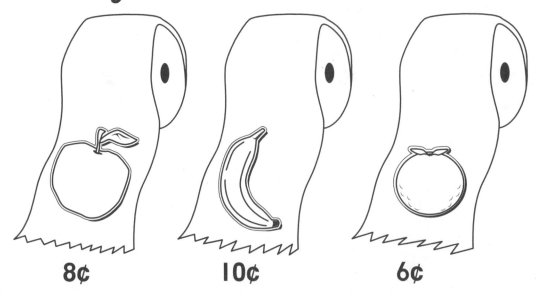

8¢   10¢   6¢

Matt drew 9 things.

He drew some ♥ and some ★.

Show what Matt drew.

Show as many different answers as you can.

Jen had 15 .

She gave 6 to Ana.

She gave 5 to Belina.

How many did Jen have left?

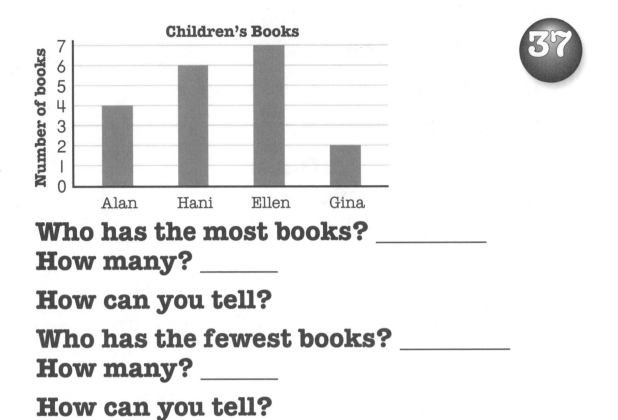

Who has the most books? _____

How many? _____

How can you tell?

Who has the fewest books? _____

How many? _____

How can you tell?

- -

Tell two ways to find the sum of these numbers.

$$1 \quad 2 \quad 3$$
$$3 \quad 2 \quad 1$$

Which way do you like best?

Why?

Put numbers in the shapes.

Put the same number in the same shapes.

$\square$ + $\bigcirc$ = 12

$\square$ + $\square$ = 6

$\square$ = _____ $\bigcirc$ = _____

- -

Walk around your classroom with a friend.

Count 2 points for each window.
_____ points

Count 5 points for each door.
_____ points

Counts 3 points for each bookcase.
_____ points

Compare the points you got with other friends.

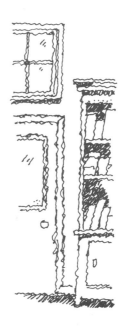

This is an *array* of 12 chips.

It has 3 rows.

There are 4 chips in each row.

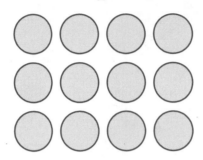

Draw other arrays of 12 chips.

Tell how many rows.

Tell how many chips in each row.

- -

Play Dots with a friend. Take turns.

Roll 3 🎲 . Count the dots.

The player with more dots wins.

Play Dots 10 times.

Who won more times?

Are there more apples or more pieces of fruit?

Tell how you know.

Work with a friend.

Tell addition and subtraction stories about the playground.

Give money to Danny so he has as much as Shondra.

How much money will you give to Danny?

Shondra's Money   Danny's Money

Katie drew 2 more butterflies than flowers.

Katie drew 2 squirrels.

Find Katie's picture.

A   B   C

Draw 人 **in the table to show how many players.**

Each 人 **stands for 2 players.**

Bean-Bag Teams

Team	Number of players	Number of players
1	8	
2	12	
3	10	
4	14	

- -

Make your calculator count.

Press these buttons.

Guess the next number you will see before you press = **again.**

Start with another number.

Guess again.

Tell what you know from the graph.

Favorite Fruit

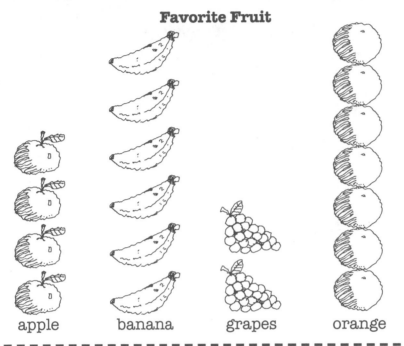

apple   banana   grapes   orange

- -

Which has more ?

Tell how you found out.

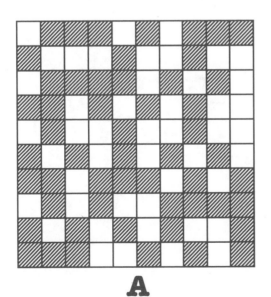

A

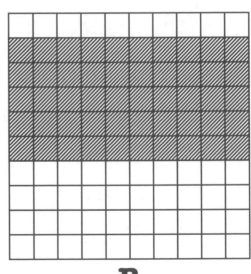

B

©Addison Wesley Longman, Inc./Published by Dale Seymour Publications®

How many squares? _____

How many circles? _____

Are there more squares or more circles? _____

How many more? _____

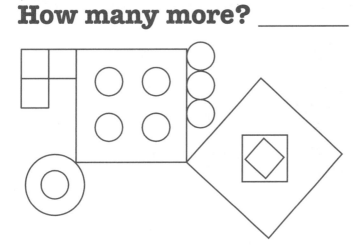

- -

Talk with a friend.

Ask questions with number answers.

Write the three questions you like best.

How many sisters do you have?

There are 3 children riding bikes.
Each rides a bicycle or a tricycle.
How many wheels can there be?

Draw 3 more animals in the picture.

Write a story about the picture.

Use numbers in your story.

Tell about all the animals.

©Addison Wesley Longman, Inc./Published by Dale Seymour Publications®

©Addison Wesley Longman, Inc./Published by Dale Seymour Publications®

There are 2 nickels in each box.

There are 5 pennies in each can.

Do you want the boxes or the cans? Tell why.

- -

How many pounds are on scale C?

How many marbles are not green?
Tell how you know.

20 Marbles
3 red   4 green
4 blue   9 yellow

Kyle had some apples.

He gave 3 to Marsha.

He gave 2 to Ang.

Kyle has I apple left.

How many apples did Kyle have before he gave some away?

Work with a friend.

Use 2 plates and 18 cubes.

Take some cubes.

Put the same number of cubes on each plate.

Write how many.

Try again.

Cubes	Plates	Cubes on each plate
	2	
	2	
	2	
	2	
	2	
	2	
	2	
	2	
	2	

The answer is 10.

What is the question?

60

Write rows 5, 6, and 7.

Row 1   1 2

Row 2   1 2 3

Row 3   1 2 3 4

Row 4   1 2 3 4 5

Row 5

Row 6

Row 7

What is the last number in row 20?

Tell how you decided.

- -

2 grams   **3 grams**   **5 grams**

Put 4 shapes on the scale.

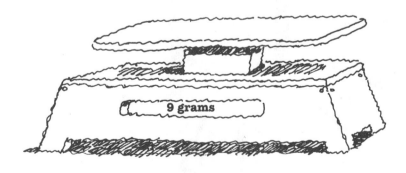

9 grams

©Addison Wesley Longman, Inc./Published by Dale Seymour Publications®

Get some pennies, nickels, and dimes.

Show all the ways to make 15¢.

Draw the coins.

penny

nickel

dime

Jay's birthday

- is after April 3.
- is before April 18.
- is a Thursday.
- is not April 11.

When is Jay's birthday?

April

S	M	T	W	T	F	S
	1	2	3	4	5	6
7	8	9	10	11	12	13
14	15	16	17	18	19	20
21	22	23	24	25	26	27
28	29	30				

Pick a plant.

Write clues.

**Have a friend use the clues
to find the plant.**

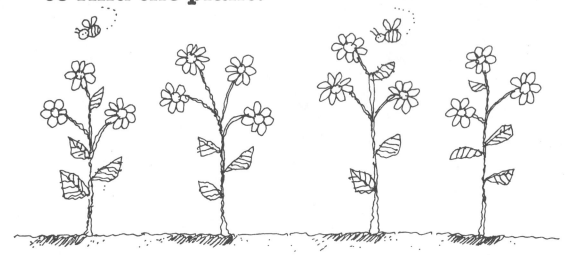

- -

How many for 6 houses?

_____ chimneys   _____ windows

_____ doors

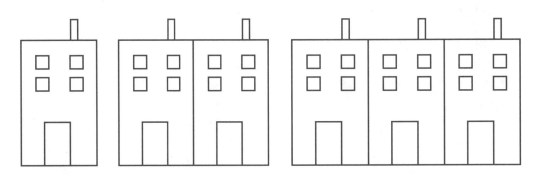

1 house	2 houses	3 houses
1 chimney	2 chimneys	3 chimneys
4 windows	8 windows	12 windows
1 door	2 doors	3 doors

©Addison Wesley Longman, Inc./Published by Dale Seymour Publications®

©Addison Wesley Longman, Inc./Published by Dale Seymour Publications®

You have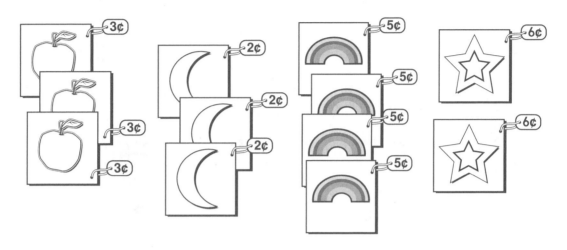

67

Which stickers would you buy?

Start at the bottom of the graph.
Color a square for each shape.

68

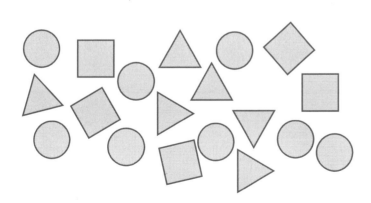

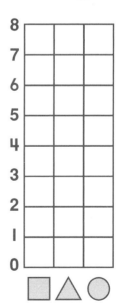

Tell a story about the graph.

Carla eats 2 cookies.

Lea eats 3 more cookies than Carla.

How many cookies are left?

Make up ages to fit the facts.

Facts

- Nigel is the oldest.
- Tina is older than Theo.
- Mara is younger than Theo.

| years old | years old | years old | years old |

Write names next to the pictures.

Write heights that make sense.

Tomas is taller than Luke.

Jeff is taller than Tomas.

Bonnie, Ang, and Pedro each pick the same number of flowers.

How many flowers does each person pick?

Tell how you know.

There are 6 dogs.

How many

- tails? _____

- eyes? _____

- noses? _____

- legs? _____

73

- -

There are 5 children in the Rizzo family.

74

I have the same number of brothers as sisters.

How many children are girls?

What animal will be on car 30?
Tell how you know.

Write a letter on each coin.

- Write P for a penny.

- Write N for a nickel.

- Write D for a dime.

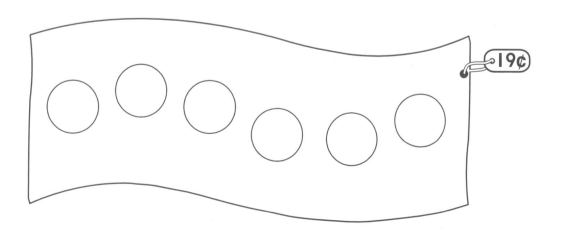

You want 8 party hats.

Find all the ways you can buy exactly 8 hats. Make a list.

package of 3

package of 2

package of 4

- -

Put numbers in the story.

The story must make sense.

Joel is _____ years old.

Rosa is Joel's younger sister. She is _____ years old.

Joel is _____ years older than Rosa.

Bill is _____ years older than Joel.

Bill is _____ years old.

This is a – 3 pattern.

Fill in the numbers.

100, 97, 94, ___, 88,

___ , ___ , ___ , ___ , ___

Make up a – pattern.

Start with 60.

Give it to a friend to finish.

60, ___ , ___ , ___ , ___ ,

___ , ___ , ___

- -

**Mighty Mason did
l pull-up on Monday.**

**He did 3 more on Tuesday
than on Monday.**

**He did 3 more each day
than the day before.**

**How many pull-ups did
he do on Friday?**

There are 8 raisins in all.

There are 2 fewer raisins on one plate than on the other.

Draw the raisins.

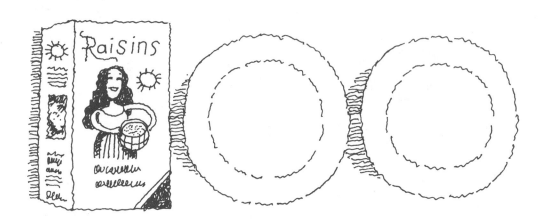

- -

Which number is greater?

- The number of teachers in your school.

- The number of boys in your school.

Why do you think so?

Which number am I?

- I am greater than 25.

- I have more ones than tens.

- I am less than 70.

89

25

48

31

penny

nickel

dime

Juan has 2 coins.

They are pennies, nickels, or dimes.

How much money does Juan have?

How many answers can you find?

Make a list.

Sort these numbers into 2 groups.

2   5   4   25

8   45   12

18   26   15

Tell how the numbers in each group are alike.

- -

Count by fives to 100.

Count by tens to 100.

Do you say more numbers when you count by fives or by tens?

Tell how you know.

What is my secret number?

Clues

- It is less than 15.
- You say it when you count by fours.
- You say it when you count by threes.

My secret number is _____.

87

Work with a friend.

Each of you write 3 numbers with more tens than ones.

Who wrote the greatest number? Circle it.

Who wrote the least number? Put an X on it.

88

Write the numbers in the blanks.

Make sure the numbers make sense.

Maggie is _____ years old.

She weighs _____ pounds.

She has _____ cat.

She lives at _____ Main Street.

45

1   5   726

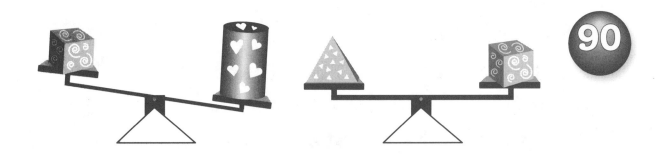

The  weighs 6 pounds.

What could be the weight of the ▨ **?**

What could be the weight of the ▲ **?**

Tell how you decided.

Think about things in your home.
Write names in the blanks.

There is 1 _____ in my home.

There are fewer than
5 _____ in my home.

There are more than
10 _____ in my home.

There are more than
100 _____ in my home.

- -

Play with a friend. Take turns.

Pick 2 numbers from the Number Box. Add.

Find the sum on the Game Board. Color it.

Number Box

20	
	10
40	
	60
30	

Game Board

50	60	90
40	free	80
30	100	70

Try to get 3 in a row: →↓↘ or ↗.

What number am I?

- I am less than 70.

- I am more than 25.

- I have less than 6 tens.

- I have more ones than tens.

52   23   87

34   69   18

Make up a number rule.

Write the numbers that fit the rule in the circle.

Write the other numbers outside the circle.

Have a friend guess your rule.

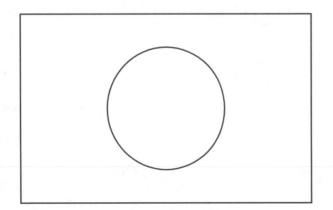

I have one beak.

I have two eyes.

Finish the lists.

Tell what comes in ones and twos.

Comes in Ones	Comes in Twos
1. noses	1. shoes
2.	2.
3.	3.
4.	4.
5.	5.

- -

Jerry took half of these carrots:

Chris took half of these carrots:

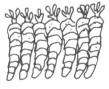

Who has more carrots?
Tell how you know.

Work with a friend.

Make a mark for each object in your class.

Then find the totals.

total: _____	total: _____	total: _____	total: _____

Check your totals with other friends.

- -

Riva wrote the numbers 1 to 99.

How many 3s did Riva write in the ones place?

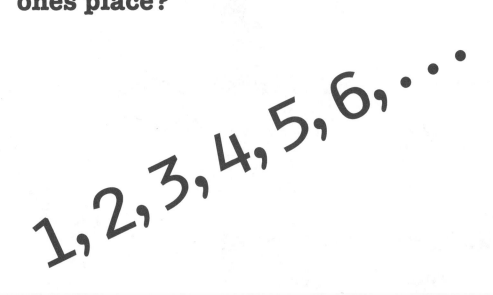

Play with a friend. Take turns.

Pick 2 numbers from the Number Box. Subtract.

Color the difference on the Game Board.

Number Box

80	
	10
40	
	30
90	

Game Board

20	60	30
40	free	80
50	10	70

Try to get 3 in a row: → ↓ ↘ or ↗

Work with a friend.

Fill in the missing numbers.

1	2	3	4	5	
			15	16	17
		25			
33					

Answers

1. B

2. Possible answers: Count by ones. Count by twos and count on 1. See 8 and count on 1. Count on ones from 5. Count back 1 from 10.

3. 7

4. Methods will vary. Connecting each banana to a monkey shows the one-to-one correspondence.

5. Possible answer: The snowman has 1 hat, 2 eyes, 1 nose, 1 scarf, 2 sticks (arms), 3 "fingers" on each "hand," and 5 buttons.

6. 9

7.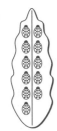

8. D

9. 6

10. 8; Explanations will vary.

11. Answers will vary.

12. Stories will vary.

13. 18

14. Answers will vary. C should have fewer than A, and A should have fewer than B.

15. 10

16. Story problems will vary.

17. 3

18. 6, 8, 3, 5; Questions will vary.

19. Answers will vary.

20. Line placements will vary. There must be 6 stars on each side.

21. 435, 25, 4

22. Lists will vary.

23. Answers will vary.

24. 18

26. B

27. Stories will vary.

28. Answers will vary.

29. Answers will vary.

30. 1, 5, 9, 13, 17, 21, 25, 29, 33, 37; Patterns will vary.

31. 7

32. Answers will vary.

33. Answers will vary.

34. no; 2 bananas and 1 apple cost 28¢.

35. Possible answers:
    8 ♥, 1 ★;   7 ♥, 2 ★;   6 ♥, 3 ★;
    5 ♥, 4 ★;   4 ♥, 5 ★;   3 ♥, 6 ★;
    2 ♥, 7 ★;   1 ♥, 8 ★

36. 4

37. Ellen, 7, tallest bar; Gina, 2, shortest bar

38. Possible answers: Add each column and then add: 4 + 4 + 4. *Or* add each row and double: 6 + 6. *Or* add 2 + 3 and 2 + 3 to get 10, and add 1 + 1 to get 2; then 10 + 2 = 12. *Or* count on.

39. 3, 9

40. Answers will vary.

41. Possible answers: 12 rows of 1, 6 rows of 2, 4 rows of 3, 2 rows of 6, 1 row of 12

43. More pieces of fruit. Apples and bananas are fruit. There are 9 pieces of fruit and 5 apples.

44. Stories will vary.

45. 5¢ (1 nickel or 5 pennies)

46. B

47. The table should show 4, 6, 5, and 7 stick figures, respectively.

48. 50; Other sequences will vary.

49. Possible answers: Four people chose apple, 6 chose banana, 2 chose grapes, and 7 chose orange. *Or* orange is the favorite, grapes are the least favorite. *Or* more people chose banana than apple.

50. A; Explanations will vary.

51. 7; 9; circles; 2

52. Questions will vary.

53. Possible answers: 9, 8, 7, 6

54. Pictures and stories will vary.

55. For more money, take the boxes. There is 40¢ in the boxes and 25¢ in the cans.

56. 19 pounds

57. 16; Explanations will vary.

58. 6

59. Tables will vary. Possible answers: 18, 9; 16, 8; 14, 7; 12, 6; 10, 5; 8, 4; 6, 3; 4, 2; 2, 1.

60. Questions will vary.

61. Row 5 1 2 3 4 5 6
    Row 6 1 2 3 4 5 6 7
    Row 7 1 2 3 4 5 6 7 8
    21; The last number in each row is 1 more than the row number.

62. Drawing should show 1 pyramid and 3 spheres.

63. 1 dime, 1 nickel; 1 dime, 5 pennies; 3 nickels; 2 nickels, 5 pennies; 1 nickel, 10 pennies; 15 pennies

64. April 4

65. Clues will vary, but might indicate the number of flowers, leaves, and bees.

66. 6 chimneys, 24 windows, 6 doors

67. Answers will vary, but the cost must be 12¢ or less.

68. The graph should show 5 squares, 6 triangles, and 8 circles. Stories will vary.

69. 3

70. Ages will vary. From youngest to oldest they must be Mara, Theo, Tina, and Nigel.

71. Heights will vary. From shortest to tallest they must be Luke, Tomas, and Jeff.

72. 7; Answers will vary.

73. 6, 12, 6, 24

74. 3

75. pig; Explanations will vary.

76. 1 dime, 1 nickel, 4 pennies

77. 2 packs of 4; 1 pack of 4 and 2 packs of 2; 2 packs of 3 and 1 pack of 2; 4 packs of 2

78. Answers will vary. From youngest to oldest they are Rosa, Joel, and Bill.

79. 100, 97, 94, 91, 88, 85, 82, 79, 76, 73; Patterns will vary.

80. 13

81. Drawing should show 5 raisins on one plate and 3 on the other.

82 Answers will vary.

83. 48

84. 20¢ (2 dimes), 15¢ (dime, nickel),
     11¢ (dime, penny), 10¢ (2 nickels),
     6¢ (nickel, penny), 2¢ (2 pennies)

85. Some possible groups are even vs.
     odd, multiplies of twos vs. multiples
     of fives, one-digit vs. two-digit
     numbers, and over 20 vs. under 20.

86. by fives; When you count by fives,
     you say all the tens *and* all the
     numbers with fives in the ones
     place.

87. 12

88. Answers will vary.

89. 5, 45, 1, 726

90. Answers will vary. The box could
     weigh any number of pounds less
     than the can because the can is
     heavier. The pyramid weighs the
     same as the box because they
     balance.

91. Answers will vary.

93. 34

94. Rules will vary.

95. Lists will vary.

96. Chris has more; Jerry has 6 carrots
     and Chris has 7.

97. Answers will vary.

98. 10

100. The missing numbers from left to
      right and top to bottom are 7, 13,
      14, 26, 34, and 35.